W9-CBD-782

SIGNSPOTTING 4

THE ART OF MISCOMMUNICATION

Compiled by Doug Lansky

A PERIGEE BOOK

A PERIGEE BOOK
Published by the Penguin Group
Penguin Group (USA) Inc.
375 Hudson Street, New York, New York 10014, USA
Penguin Group (Canada), 90 Eglinton Avenue East, Suite 700,
Toronto, Ontario M4P 2Y3, Canada
(a division of Pearson Penguin Canada Inc.)
Penguin Books Ltd., 80 Strand, London WC2R 0RL, England
Penguin Group Ireland, 25 St. Stephen's Green, Dublin 2, Ireland
(a division of Penguin Books Ltd.)
Penguin Group (Australia), 250 Camberwell Road, Camberwell,
Victoria 3124, Australia (a division of Pearson Australia Group Pty. Ltd.)
Penguin Books India Pvt. Ltd., 11 Community Centre,
Panchsheel Park, New Delhi—110 017, India
Penguin Group (NZ), 67 Apollo Drive, Rosedale, Auckland 0632,
New Zealand (a division of Pearson New Zealand Ltd.)
Penguin Books (South Africa) (Pty.) Ltd., 24 Sturdee Avenue,
Rosebank, Johannesburg 2196, South Africa

Penguin Books Ltd., Registered Offices: 80 Strand,
London WC2R 0RL, England

While the author has made every effort to provide accurate
telephone numbers and Internet addresses at the time of
publication, neither the publisher nor the author assumes any
responsibility for errors or for changes that occur after publication.
Further, the publisher does not have any control over and does not
assume any responsibility for author or third-party websites or their
content.

Copyright © 2011 by Doug Lansky

All rights reserved.
No part of this book may be reproduced, scanned, or distributed in
any printed or electronic form without permission. Please do not
participate in or encourage piracy of copyrighted materials in
violation of the author's rights. Purchase only authorized editions.
PERIGEE is a registered trademark of Penguin Group (USA) Inc.
The "P" design is a trademark belonging to Penguin Group (USA)
Inc.

First edition: September 2011

Library of Congress Cataloging-in-Publication Data

Signspotting 4 : the art of miscommunication / compiled by Doug
Lansky.— 1st ed.
    p.   cm.
  ISBN 978-0-399-53614-4
  1. Signs and signboards—Pictorial works. 2. Billboards—Pictorial
works. 3. Travel—Humor. 4. Photography, Humorous. I. Lansky,
Doug. II. Title: Signspotting four. III. Title: Sign spotting four.
  GT3910.S543   2011
  659.13'42—dc22   2011014077

PRINTED IN MEXICO

10   9   8   7   6   5   4   3   2   1

Most Perigee books are available at special quantity discounts for
bulk purchases for sales promotions, premiums, fund-raising, or
educational use. Special books, or book excerpts, can also be
created to fit specific needs. For details, write: Special Markets,
Penguin Group (USA) Inc., 375 Hudson Street, New York, New York
10014.

To the signspotters.
They not only are alert international travelers but also possess the winning combination of a sense of humor and a camera.

INTRODUCTION

One of the strangest things about signs is how easily we miss them—impressive considering the imposing size, bright colors, and the fact that they're placed almost directly in our line of sight. Doesn't seem to matter if we're on foot, biking, or driving—we zip right past them. The reason is that most of us live in a sign forest. That is, our environment is littered with signs clamoring for attention. In Tom Vanderbilt's fascinating book *Traffic: Why We Drive the Way We Do*, he examines numerous studies on driving behavior, and has an interesting section on our observational skills. In one study, for example, "researchers pulled over drivers on the highway and asked them if they recalled having seen certain traffic signs. The recall rates were as low as 20 percent." So what did they recall in that 20 percent? It wasn't necessarily the biggest or brightest signs . . . I'll tell you the answer in a minute.

Before we get to our selective memory, I thought it better to cover the factors that determine what signs we *see*. For starters, Vanderbilt explained, it can depend on how experienced we are at driving (and this would presumably apply to biking as well). Studies showed that newbie drivers were so focused on just staying in their lane and maintaining the correct speed that they spent much more time looking straight ahead and used much less peripheral vision. The more experience we get, the better our peripheral vision gets.

Other things reduce peripheral vision: driving fast, snow or rain, obstacles, and aggressive drivers around us. These aren't particularly surprising. More interesting, though, is if we're talking on the phone. The "hundred-car study" mentioned in Vanderbilt's book showed that when experienced drivers got on their cell phones, they "began to look almost exclusively straight ahead, much more so than they did when they were not on their cell phones." This also holds true outside the car. Vanderbilt mentioned a study in Finland where "pedestrians using mobile devices walked more slowly and were less able to interact with the device, pausing occasionally to 'sample the environment.'"

In addition to peripheral vision and distractions, there's familiarity. The closer we are to home or work (that is, the better we know an area) the more likely we are to ignore the signs. Why? We know which signs are there; chances are we stopped reading them long ago. Same goes for very familiar signs. We recognize the shape, size, and color and make a quick connection without having to read it. Carl Andersen, a vision specialist at the Federal Highway Administration, told Vanderbilt about a study in which they intentionally misspelled "stop" on a red stop sign. After drivers stopped, then drove off, researchers asked them about the sign. The vast majority never noticed the misspelling.

Here's another case that hits a little closer to home: I had an Australian traveler show me his copy of *Signspotting*. He had it open to a page that had a roadside billboard ad for McDonald's. "This sign is right by my house," he said. "I pass it every day. I don't understand why you included it in your book. What's so funny about it?" The sign, typical for McDonald's, had a big yellow McDonald's "M" right in front of the town's name, which happened to be Yass. It didn't take much imagination to read the sign as "MYass." I asked him to read it to me out loud. The penny dropped.

This is how so many signspotting misses occur. Most of us presume that signs are spelled correctly and are not riddled with double entendres or strange messages. The other reason people walk by these funny signs all the time—and here comes the answer to the low-level cliff-hanger—is that the 20 percent of signs that drivers recalled were the signs "drivers judged most important." This includes things like the speed limit, relevant exits, and an upcoming rest stop. Our brain makes a snap judgment based on a cursory glance, whether it's important or informational clutter not worth closer inspection.

Now that you think about all the ways in which we commonly miss funny signs, it's amazing we manage to catch them at all.

It also explains why so many signspottings are captured by travelers. Consider the advantages. They're not likely to see familiar signs, so all signs become potentially important and worthy of closer inspection. They're more likely on foot and actively observing their surroundings. They're not as likely to use their mobile phones when abroad. Plus, they're carrying a camera and have time to stop.

Chances are you've already passed right by one or more of the 1,000+ signs in the Signspotting book series without ever realizing it (and you probably did it in your hometown). If you want to start spotting more funny signs, it's pretty simple: Adopt the mind-set of a traveler. Slow down and look around. And when you do see one, please send it to Signspotting.com so others can enjoy it as well.

LOCATION: ADANWOMASE, GHANA   CREDIT: PATRICK SMITH

LOCATION: BUSHMILLS, NORTHERN IRELAND   CREDIT: TONY WHEELER

Nothing quite says "happy" like getting a giant syringe hammered into your ass.

I bet this cash machine is popular.

LOCATION: ROCHE, SWITZERLAND   CREDIT: JEAN-PIERRE JORDAN

The murder of the stick figure was captured by this detailed artist rendering.

LOCATION: PITTSBURGH, PENNSYLVANIA, USA   CREDIT: JEN HENSLER

And let me guess . . . turning the key activates the lock.

LOCATION: ANCHORAGE, ALASKA, USA   CREDIT: DUANE MAGOON

Clever business model. Wonder where they got the cell phones . . .

LOCATION: GLASGOW, SCOTLAND   CREDIT: ILENIA

An early pictogram for the guillotine.

LOCATION: KOH SAMUI, THAILAND   CREDIT: ALAN MCKEE

Are you pregnant? Do you have an
ear in need of cleaning? Or a motorbike?
We can help.

DANGER

MILITARY TARGET AREA

DO NOT TOUCH ANYTHING

IT MAY EXPLODE

AND KILL YOU

LOCATION: CHRISTCHURCH, NEW ZEALAND   CREDIT: ANNE BIELAMOWICZ

And then you'd be dead. And you wouldn't like that too much, would you?
Would you?! Didn't think so.

LOCATION: THAILAND   CREDIT: JONATHAN WEISS

When you think of Elephant Dung Factory, the first thing that probably comes to mind is, How can I get some of this enormous shit home to share with friends and family? (The second thing is, Elephant dung is made in a factory?)

LOCATION: SHANGHAI, CHINA   CREDIT: DOROTHY BIRNER

Let's go to the Old Town and perhaps have—or perhaps not—a snack.

LOCATION: ELMINA, GHANA   CREDIT: PATRICK SMITH

More great marital advice inside!

LOCATION: MIAMI, FLORIDA, USA   CREDIT: ALISON BOURDEAU

Nice to see the porn industry has an official headquarters.

LOCATION: STOCKHOLM, SWEDEN   CREDIT: JENNIFER PETERSON

In Swedish, *Tisdagar* means "Tuesdays" and "Poetry Gangbang" means . . . well, your guess is as good as mine.

LOCATION: YANGSHUO, CHINA   CREDIT: RASMUS BAK

LOCATION: GREAT FALLS, VIRGINIA, USA   CREDIT: ANNE BIELAMOWICZ

A giant leap for mankind!

Messiah-free zone.

LOCATION: DELRAY BEACH, FLORIDA, USA   CREDIT: LON ENGLAND

Vegetables only today. Fruit has priority on even days of the month.

LOCATION: ENGLAND   CREDIT: RUSSELL BOWTON

The English have their priorities right!

LOCATION: SOUTH AFRICA   CREDIT: MATTHEW JONES

LOCATION: SVENDBORG, DENMARK   CREDIT: THOMAS WOLL

Oh no, he didn't land there.

You may be attacked by a savage wolf, but otherwise the toilet is wheelchair friendly.

小心碰头
Watch Your Herd

LOCATION: ZHAOQING, CHINA   CREDIT: GEORGE LOUIE

A practical reminder for all those people wandering around the city with a herd.

LOCATION: GUANGZHOU, CHINA   CREDTI: LYNN IHLENFELDT

Presumably that text is Chinese for "Go ahead, make a left turn from the right lane . . . we dare you."

ไปบางซื่อ
To Bang Sue

2
ชานชาลา
Platform

LOCATION: BANGKOK, THAILAND   CREDIT: RONALD WINDY

Guess that means you won't be the first.

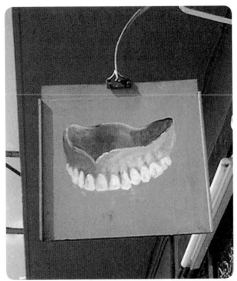

LOCATION: MARRAKESH, MOROCCO   CREDIT: PATRICK SMITH

You'll have to find someone else to work on your lower teeth.

LOCATION: WALPOLE, HEW HAMPSHIRE, USA   CREDIT: MICHAEL DRURY

Where the deer and (presumably antelope) register to play.

LOCATION: HALIFAX, NOVA SCOTIA, CANADA   CREDIT: BRUCE MARTIN

First, we'll park your car. And then we'll put in a ventricular catheter and bypass your malfunctioning arachnoidal granulations and get that excess fluid drained before you can say, "Where's my valet ticket?"

LOCATION: LAURINBURG, NORTH CAROLINA, USA   CREDIT: ETHEL F. RAINWATER

What happens when a porn star retires on a hobby farm.

LOCATION: JAMAICA   CREDIT: ELMERROZE

Hard to say if they're taking a crack at the local work ethic or they're having a speeding issue with a visiting '80s Australian band.

NO-CAUGHT-IN-BETWEEN ZONE

LOCATION: NASHVILLE, TENNESSEE, USA   CREDIT: LOLA WHITE

Perhaps the only zone of its kind.

Please,

NO CLIMBING ON COW.

Thank you.

LOCATION: CHARLOTTETOWN, CALIFORNIA, USA   CREDIT: ROBERT MOISOFF

Running and jumping on cow only.

LOCATION: CAIRNS, AUSTRALIA   CREDIT: CORINNE FORDSCHMID

Stay alert!

LOCATION: FT. COLLINS, COLORADO, USA   CREDIT: SUSAN GIBBS

Lemme guess . . . they also have an endless parking lot (max: 23 cars) and an all-you-can-eat buffet (max: 1.5 pounds per person).

THE NEW WOW FACTOR

Go online and look up "sign making" and "strategy," and you'll find a surprising amount of free advice for would-be sign makers. They talk about first impressions, branding, simplicity, uniformity, the "wow factor," demographics, lasting impressions, and the fact that the average reader will only have four to ten seconds to absorb your message. All extremely interesting and helpful stuff.

I think it's a pretty safe assumption that the bulk of the sign makers whose work appears in this book managed to neglect just about every essential element. They did, however, discover a new category: the unintentional wow factor. This may be even more powerful than an intentional wow factor, which leads to a longer-lasting impression, stronger branding, and will have readers staring at it for more then the standard four to ten seconds. If it wasn't quite so embarrassing, it would be marketing genius.

LOCATION: LA CHAUX-DE-FONDS, SWITZERLAND CREDIT: STEFAN MEMMINGER

So they do test bikinis! And to think for all these years no one took those college students with "Bikini Tester" T-shirts seriously.

WILD LIFE
MAINTENANCE
SHOP

13

LOCATION: MALCOM, NEBRASKA, USA   CREDIT: BILL JONES

Fur changed, stripes realigned, antlers replaced . . . preferably every two years or 30,000 miles.

LOCATION: SLITE, SWEDEN   CREDIT: CATHARINA COYLE

Apparently, "Utter Crap Café" was already taken.

WWW.THEHEALTHDEPARTMENT.ORG

STAUNTON-AUGUSTA
HEALTH DEPARTMENT
BREASTFEEDING
A VITAL EMERGENCY   RESPONSE
ARE   YOU   READY ?

LOCATION: STAUNTON, VIRGINA, USA   CREDIT: LAURA LASTER

Okay, it's an emergency. We need a response. Everyone get ready to lactate!

LOCATION: BATMAN, TURKEY   CREDIT: MARINA KHONINA

Havaalani is indeed Turkish for "airport." So now you know where the superhero prefers to land.

立入禁止
この土地は売物件ではありません

LOCATION: KYOTO, JAPAN   CREDIT: THOMAS HOLLAND

It's not often you see the "Keep Out!" skull and crossbones translated into a kid-friendly version. Or a Valentine's Day version.

LOCATION: OHIO, USA   CREDIT: SARAH BOYSEL

LOCATION: EIN KAREM, ISRAEL   CREDIT: DIANA BUTLER

See how thoughtful they are? Those hunters are always thinking about safety.

Psssst, don't do any of this stuff. And remember, it's a secret.

LOCATION: GIZA, EGYPT   CREDIT: JACKSON BUCHANAN

Motto: "We get you there. You find your own way home."

LOCATION: HELSINGØR (ELSINORE), DENMARK   CREDIT: MAJA GABELGAARD NIELSEN

The exciting sequel to *I, Robot*.

LOCATION: FAIRMONT, WEST VIRGINIA, USA   CREDIT: RYAN HUFFMAN

LOCATION: MINNEAPOLIS, MINNESOTA, USA   CREDIT: JOSE J. GONZALEZ

Finally, a special lane for indecisive drivers.

Ahem, that's a bit awkward.

Look, a giant hole in the middle of the road. Surprise!

LOCATION: ABU DHABI, UNITED ARAB EMIRATES
CREDIT: BARIS SEVER

How exactly are you supposed to behave in a monkey zone, other than perhaps not eating bananas in public?

LOCATION: THAILAND
CREDIT: MICHELE MARTIN

The much-anticipated sequel to *Man vs. Wild.*

LOCATION: HONG KONG
CREDIT: JAY DAVIDSON

LOCATION: KILL, IRELAND   CREDIT: INGELA GUSTAVSSON

Hardest decision was picking the Kill High School mascot.
Do you go with the grim reaper, Freddy Krueger, Hannibal Lecter, or a Kamikaze pilot?

快速通道
仅限小便
违者重罚
Express Lane
For urinating only!

LOCATION: BEIJING, CHINA   CREDIT: KELLY JEAN DUNN

It's about time an express lane was set up for this. Well done, China!

LOCATION: OREGON, USA   CREDIT: CHRIS ALLAN

Might want to check with the tourist board before you make that the official motto.

本厕所已经加强清洁
请安心使用马桶坐垫

LOCATION: TAICHUNG, TAIWAN   CREDIT: SHARON WONG

You made it all the way to the bathroom. Hope it's not too much to ask you to hold it for another 12 inches.

Kui **viskad** prügi maha ja peidad prahti sinna, kuhu see ei kuulu, siis reostad sa otseselt sedasama maailma, mis varsti saab su oma **lapse** elupaigaks. Aga kas tema ei väärigi puhast elukeskkonda? Kui sa sellest aru ei saa, siis oleks ju ausam panna ta kohe elama **prügikasti**?

LOCATION: PARNU, ESTONIA   CREDIT: TONY WHEELER

LOCATION: RAJASTHAN, INDIA   CREDIT: DAN O'BRIEN

And without the bathwater!

Nothing beats a cold bear on a hot day.
Just try not to wake him.

47

LOCATION: PANAMA CITY, PANAMA   CREDIT: MEGAN KIMBLE

Last one in the water is a steriod-saturated muscle head.

LOCATION: NEWCASTLE, AUSTRALIA   CREDIT: KIM PITINGOLO

Bird swooping is the leading cause
of bird-related injuries.

クマはどこにでもいます。

見つけても絶対に
プロレスをしない。
タックルをしない。

LOCATION: FUJIKYU HIGHLAND PARK, MT. FUJI, JAPAN   CREDIT: DANIEL PEEL

We know you're tempted to just walk up and
punch a bear in the nose. We feel that way all
the time. But please, just this once, we ask
you to make peace.

49

LOCATION: HONG KONG   CREDIT: INDIRA WEIRINGA

That's one way to divide up society: all octopi to the left and people who
need change on the right. I imagine this clears things up quite a bit. Before it must
have been a giant mess with tentacles and loose change all over the place.

LOCATION: NAPLES, ITALY   CREDIT: LACHLAN MURRAY

"Welcome to Nasti Customer Service. Please wait until the next Nasti representative is available to help you."

メロディペットはここまで！

The melody pet is to here !

LOCATION: HAKONE, JAPAN   CREDIT: JESS AMMANN

They might have also translated it this way: "Here pet, the melody is to!"
Or maybe: "Pet the melody to is here!" Personally, I prefer: "Melody is the pet, here to!"

LOCATION: MILAN, ITALY   CREDIT: DALE KUSHNER

LOCATION: CANBERRA, AUSTRALIA   CREDIT: MICHELLE GRAYSON

Nothing like the love between a dog
and his owner.

Nice to see an employer with the guts
to set some high standards.

小心落水
Care fell into the water

LOCATION: THREE GORGES DAM, CHINA   CREDIT: CAROL HUGHES

Then Happiness and Love jumped in after.

LOCATION: CAIRO, EGYPT   CREDIT: AMY LENTZ

Free range is nice: Kobe beef cows
can live in luxury, but in Egypt they have
a chance to pursue a PhD.

LOCATION: COPENHAGEN, DENMARK   CREDIT: MARTHA DEBELAK

Just to be safe, best to hold off on
the beans for the next 10 miles.

UNWEAR THE SLIPPERS
AND SHOES

LOCATION: KYAINGTONG, MYANMAR CREDIT: RUSSELL COHEN

And then when you return you can un-leave them here.

LOCATION: MONTEREY, CALIFORNIA, USA   CREDIT: DENNIS BLASIUS

LOCATION: LEATHERHEAD, UNITED KINGDOM   CREDIT: MILA FERRAMOSCA

But they're so yummy. Mom, can't we please have just one more racoon dropping?

Pssst, Al Gore . . . here it is.

موقف

٢٤ ساعه فقط

PARKING

24 Hrs. ONLY

LOCATION: MANAMA, BAHRAIN   CREDIT: ERIN PISCHKE

Tough new parking restrictions.

LOCATION: WILKINSBURG, PENNSYLVANIA, USA   CREDIT: ANNE MORRIS

Another contestant for "Most Obvious Sign" award.

LOCATION: CARMEL, INDIANA, USA   CREDIT: CHRIS BOWMAN

A Valentine's Day dream dinner come true.

non salire o scendere
durante la chiusura

LOCATION: MILAN, ITALY   CREDIT: JOEL WATTS

If only stick figures had their own funniest home video show . . .

LOCATION: NEAR HOKATIKA, NEW ZEALAND   CREDIT: JOHN HUNTER

Semi-rotten horse poo for sale? There's an untapped business idea.

好食道

SMART NOSHERY MAKES YOU SLOBBER

SMART NOSHERY MAKES YOU SLOBBER 好食道

SMART NOSHERY MAKES YOU S

LOCATION: SHANGHAI, CHINA   CREDIT: JOAN HEENAHAN

Finally someone willing to speak truth to power. Or noshery to slobber. Whatever.

LOCATION: VANCOUVER, CANADA   CREDIT: JENNIFER WOOD

Was going to do a double gainer with a half twist, but the toilet diving appears to have been canceled. Possibly because someone stuffed giant arrows into the toilet.

LOCATION: SWEDEN CREDIT: FREDRIK LARSSON

LOCATION: CORPUS CHRISTI, TEXAS, USA CREDIT: JEANNE A. SHEPHERD

I think we have a possible winner for "Most Graphic Dismemberment of a Stick Figure."

Don't bring your waste to just anyone. Bring it to a name you can trust.

LOCATION: HEREFORD, ENGLAND   CREDIT: JEROEN SMEETS

Be careful, those pedestrians look dangerous.

LOCATION: EUGENE, OREGON, USA   CREDIT: SHANE LEWIS

What happens when an orphanage gets an overzealous marketing director.

ходить по крышам куртин и бастионов

LOCATION: ST. PETERSBURG, RUSSIA   CREDIT: ED ABRAMS

This sign has probably averted countless suicides by large-nosed, overweight cartoonish men.

LOCATION: NICE, FRANCE   CREDIT: CHRIS TOWNSEND

Didn't think about it before, but I suppose this must be how the Tooth Fairy gets around.

DANGER

CARS RUN
RED LIGHTS!

WESTBURY HOMEOWNERS ASSOCIATION

BOWLES AVE 5900 S

LOCATION: LAKEWOOD, COLORADO, USA   CREDIT: DANIEL DUFFY

This requires another sign: "Danger, cars suddenly stop for green lights in case cars run red lights."

Last one in is a Dodge Dart.

LOCATION: TAIPEI, TAIWAN
CREDIT: PAUL N. BLEY

Those Canadian deer are getting bigger every year.

LOCATION: NORTH VANCOUVER, CANADA
CREDIT: SHIRLEY PERKINS

What to expect when you're not expecting.

LOCATION: OUTSIDE GRAND MARAIS, MINNESOTA, USA
CREDIT: TOM LOOSMORE

70

Harsh potato
フライドポテト

卵 Egg	乳製品 Milk product	そば Buckwheat	小麦 Wheat
甲殻類（えび・かに） Shellfish（Prawn・Crab）		ピーナッツ Peanut	大豆 Soy bean

VEGETARIAN MENU

LOCATION: NARITA, JAPAN   CREDIT: MARIKO BABA

Approach with caution.

LOCATION: SANTA FE, NEW MEXICO, USA   CREDIT: DELMAR PATTON

QUI SERVIZIO SENZA CODE

LOCATION: SORRENTO, ITALY   CREDIT: NEIL WILD

Nothing like the calming, whisper-like sound of a train charging by 6 feet away.

No dickheads!

สมาคมคนตาบอดจังหวัดพิษณุโ

PHITSANULOKE ASSOCIATION OF THE BLAND

LOCATION: PHITSANULOKE, THAILAND   CREDIT: JANET OTT

Not sure why the bland of Phitsanuloke have created an association,
but you know it's a rich language when they have a single word for it.

SAD DECOR
Fournitures pour peintres
DETA

RIDEAUX - SIEGES
TENTURES MURALES

PAPIERS-PEINTS
MOQUETTES

LOCATION: PARIS, FRANCE   CREDIT: GERVIS ARDOIN

We have furniture for all your depressed occasions.

LOCATION: DUBROVNIK, CROATIA   CREDIT: LARRY GITTLESON

We hope to have the country up and running again soon. Just some maintenance issues.

医疗急救室
Medical treatment dicking

LOCATION: ZHOUSHAN, CHINA   CREDIT: ANNA OLOFSSON

Hi, I'd like one of your medical dickings, please.

LOCATION: SHANGHAI, CHINA   CREDIT: RYAN O'LEARY

Don't act like you've never heard of the famous Estatua de la Libertad de Miami.

LOCATION: UMBRIA, ITALY   CREDIT: GERALDINE MCCONNELL

LOCATION: SAN FRANCISCO, CALIFORNIA, USA   CREDIT: DAVID SULLIVAN

And don't even think of coming back!

They say all good things must come to an end, but maybe this is the exception?

LOCATION: OUTSIDE MARBLE HILL, GEORGIA, USA   CREDIT: TOM KEMPPAINEN

It's now twice as close. A miracle.

LOCATION: BRISBANE, AUSTRALIA   CREDIT: LINDA ORLOFSKI

LOCATION: CURMARTHEN, WALES   CREDIT: SUSAN HARTZELL

Please observe correct crocodile visiting procedure. Or you will die.

I'd like to buy a vowel, please.

G000001

Please read the instruction leaflet carefully.
Use a condom only once .The process of the usage
does to experience personally very comfortable
unimpeded, stir up the love, increase the emotion.

请仔细阅读小盒内侧的使用说明。
本品由天然乳胶制成，每只天然胶乳橡胶避孕套只能
使用一次，所有产品均符合国际标准，有效期三年，

LOCATION: URUMQI, CHINA   CREDIT: RYAN O'LEARY

Nothing like some open and frank communication to remove the awkwardness
(and stir up the love).

LOCATION: DUBLIN, IRELAND   CREDIT: JOEY

Sure, the hats add a touch of class, but please don't blatantly stare at other men taking a crap.

LOCATION: HAARLEM, NETHERLANDS   CREDIT: JEFFREY H. SCHMITT

Smoking bad, nose-picking good.

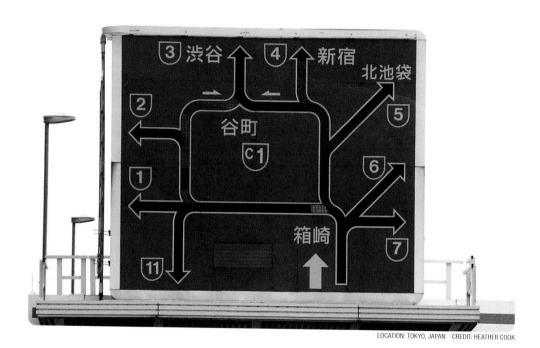

③渋谷　④新宿

北池袋

②　谷町

C1

⑤

⑥

①

箱崎

⑦

⑪

LOCATION: TOKYO, JAPAN   CREDIT: HEATHER COOK

Honey, looks like we're going to be here for a while.

D 132 6

3
4,5

MORONVILLE
ROGNON

LOCATION: BAIGNOLET, FRANCE   CREDIT: BERNARD MAPWASHIKE

For those who aren't clever enough for Margaritaville.

LOCATION: SAN FRANCISCO, CALIFORNIA, USA   CREDIT: ERIC BRODER VAN DYKE

The parking boom waits for no man.

LOCATION: DENVER, COLORADO, USA   CREDIT: ANDREA HILL

LOCATION: HONOLULU, HAWAII, USA   CREDIT: JOSEPH LEONARD

Lazy bastard husband sale is the
following week.

Newsflash!

LOCATION: BEIJING, CHINA   CREDIT: MARTIN NIELSEN

A sad commentary that so many tourists are pooping where they're not supposed to that locals had to put up a special sign for them.

LOCATION: ARIZONA   CREDIT: JIM TANNER

Next time someone tells you that you "couldn't find it with a map and a compass," just show them this photo.

It's just a small drop. Not like you're going to freefall headfirst or anything.

LOCATION: BEIJING, CHINA
CREDIT: RASMUS LARSEN

当 心 坠 落
Caution, drop down

Those Japanese mascots are getting freakier every year.

LOCATION: ANTIGUA, GUATEMALA   CREDIT: ELLIOT SANDERS

Looks like the Smithsonian is working hard to cut costs.

Darwin's theories at work. It appears these fish have adapted to the local road system.

LOCATION: SNOHOMISH, WASHINGTON, USA
CREDIT: ELAINE TOBIN

Ever wondered where traffic planners at the bottom of their class end up?

LOCATION: OMAHA, NEBRASKA, USA
CREDIT: BARBARA STUBE

Transportation department version of a quickie.

LOCATION: KONA, HAWAII, USA
CREDIT: BRIAN PLAUTZ

LOCATION: PRAGUE, CZECH REPUBLIC   CREDIT: BETH HANSING

Ever wonder what hotels do with ashtrays after they convert to a no-smoking policy? Also great for taunting smokers: "Hey, here's an ashtray you can use—NOT!"

LOCATION: MILWAUKEE, WISCONSIN, USA CREDIT: HEIDI ADRIANSEN

LOCATION: DENVER, COLORADO, USA CREDIT: OZ TWEDT

Construction workers with a sense of humor.

The air is free. To breathe. If you want to put it in your tires, it's 25 cents.

LOCATION: UNITED KINGDOM   CREDIT: MERRILL BROWN

There's an appealing combo.

LOCATION: MILWAUKEE, WISCONSIN, USA   CREDIT: MARY TATALOVICH

Hell hasn't frozen over yet, but this would appear to be the canary in the coal mine.

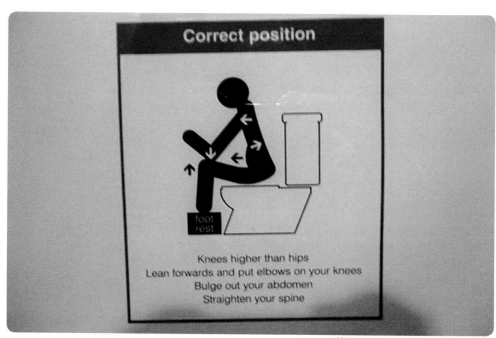

Correct position

Knees higher than hips
Lean forwards and put elbows on your knees
Bulge out your abdomen
Straighten your spine

foot rest

LOCATION: SALISBURY, ENGLAND   CREDIT: PATTY MANNING

Who knew it was so complicated?

"I said pass the ball!"

LOCATION: ATENAS, COSTA RICA
CREDIT: CAITLIN AYERS

WRONGLY WRONGED SIGNS

Yes, there are probably good explanations for several signs that don't reflect poorly on the intelligence of the sign makers. The crematorium that is offing cell phones, for example, is probably offering to collect them. The "Octopus/Change Given" sign refers, we believe, to a special subway card. But we have decided to take these and other signs at face value and simply enjoy the comic effect. As previous Signspotting books have stated, we willingly admit that if we tried to be as kind to other nations as they are to us (in terms of putting up signs in their languages), we'd surely have them rolling in the streets from laughter at our badly bungled translations. So it is with great humility that we allow ourselves a little chuckle at their expense.

LOCATION: YEREVAN, ARMENIA   CREDIT: TOM IBBOTSON

Here at the Turkish Embassy, we like to do things one by one. And by that we mean . . . well, just follow the diagram.

LOCATION: CLARK COUNTY, WISCONSIN, USA   CREDIT: JUNETTE WILKE

This is about as close as it gets to *nature's irony* with man-made road signs.

LOCATION: ULAANBAATAR, MONGOLIA   CREDIT: FREDERIC BILLOU

My hair is ruined! Thank you.

LOCATION: MURRYSVILLE, PENNSYLVANIA, USA   CREDIT: MARGARET ESHBAUGH

Talk about being born into the profession.

LOCATION: ROCKAWAY BEACH, OREGON, USA   CREDIT: LEANNE CZUPRYK

LOCATION: BEIJING, CHINA   CREDIT: VIRGINIA JARDIM

Environmentally friendly safe sex.

You're speaking too load!

LOCATION: MUNSÖ, SWEDEN   CREDIT: MONICA PERSSON

Bit of a slutty neighborhood.

LOCATION: CAIRNS, AUSTRALIA   CREDIT: KIM PITINGOLO

Please don't feed self to crocs.

LOCATION: ELDORADO, TEXAS, USA   CREDIT: DAVE DORAN

Looks like some district forgot to take their medication.

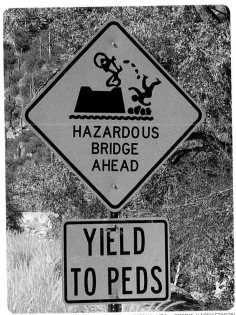

LOCATION: TUCSON, ARIZONA, USA   CREDIT: KASEY EDISON

LOCATION: CAPETOWN, SOUTH AFRICA   CREDIT: MASSIMO PERO

Only hazardous to bikers attempting to ride over the ledge.

Not much chance you're going to miss a giant hippo in the road, but just in case . . .

Please call the nurse
when you want to get off.

LOCATION: BANGKOK, THAILAND   CREDIT: MALOU DAMGAARD

Hospital care with benefits.

LOCATION: BONDA, ZIMBABWE   CREDIT: ANNE BIELAMOWICZ

Ah, the guilty pleasures of luxury travel.

LOCATION: LANTAU ISLAND, HONG KONG   CREDIT: RICH LAU

As long as you keep them at arm's length, you should be okay.

LOCATION: WATERTON LAKES, ALBERTA, CANADA   CREDIT: AL LOEBEL

LOCATION: TIROL, ITALY   CREDIT: LOUISE THISGAARD ANDERSEN

Reindeer 1, man 0.

No stepping on snails when it's raining.

LOCATION: ANTWERP, BELGIUM   CREDIT: PATRICK SMITH

"Excuse me, sir, was your meal a complete disaster?"
    "Yes, it was."
    "So happy to hear. Is there anything else, or should I bring you the bill?"

LOCATION: BALI, INDONESIA   CREDIT: MARU MATTHAEI

Anyone *not* planning on yielding to the elephant?

LOCATION: DEN HAAG, NETHERLANDS   CREDIT: ANDREW LANDSBERGEN

If you wanted to judge a society by the happiness of their wild roosters, the Dutch appear to have a clear lead.

LOCATION: MENOMONEE FALLS, WISCONSIN, USA   CREDIT: LYNN SEREBIN

So much for 30 minutes or less.

LOCATION: LIMA, PERU   CREDIT: CHRISTY MATTA

Enjoy the great taste of kraps.

LOCATION: SAINT-VALÉRY SUR SOMME, FRANCE   CREDIT: KARL CATTEEUW

Not sure what they're saying here: Please don't try to bike under the train by leaning backwards so that your back is dragging on the tire?

LOCATION: CALGARY, ALBERTA, CANADA   CREDIT: ADALAINIE

i carry your heart with me /
(i carry it in my bottle)

LOCATION: IRVING, TEXAS, USA   CREDIT: NETA MARTINEZ

From a sensitive soul patch to a slightly creepy Fu Manchu . . .
we've got all your chin hair needs covered.

115

LOCATION: IRELAND   CREDIT: ANDRÉ STÆHR

human dining
DRAEMON

LOCATION: NAGOYA, JAPAN   CREDIT: CHRISTOPHER LEPCZYK

Pssst, there's a sniper up ahead.
Don't tell anyone.

All your cannibalistic favorites.

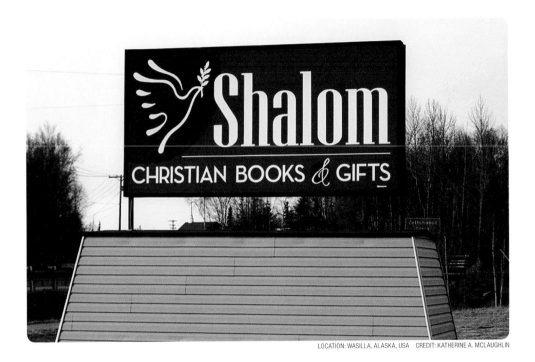

LOCATION: WASILLA, ALASKA, USA   CREDIT: KATHERINE A. MCLAUGHLIN

Or they could have gone with Hallelujah Torahs and Dreidels.

LOCATION: FISHERS, INDIANA, USA   CREDIT: RICHARD HARRIS

Perhaps discount circumcision is just a way for greenhouses to help pay the rent.

LOCATION: TRINITY, JERSEY, CHANNEL ISLANDS   CREDIT: DAVID WOODALL

LOCATION: DISNEYLAND, CALIFORNIA, USA   CREDIT: MAX WEITKAMP

This way to the only pedestrians in captivity.

Forever doesn't last as long as it used to.

LOCATION: TIGHTWAD, MISSOURI, USA   CREDIT: CHARLES RANG

LOCATION: LAS VEGAS, NEVADA, USA   CREDIT: ALEC JUNGE

Sure, you can have a loan. No problem.
How does $1.50 sound?

Thanks for the tip.

120

LOCATION: SCOTTSDALE, ARIZONA, USA   CREDIT: BILL AMUNDSON

We're your local cute and cuddly guns and ammo shop.

LOCATION: FRANCONIA, PENNSYLVANIA, USA   CREDIT: DOUGLAS CLARK

Perhaps you should make one little exception.

白切肉
Slices meat in vain

LOCATION: TAIXING, JIANGSU, CHINA   CREDIT: PETER ALAN SO

It was all carved up for naught.

LOCATION: WEST LOS ANGELES, CALIFORNIA, USA   CREDIT: CRISTYN WINGOOD

What does my dad do? Let's just say people call him "tranny man."

"This giant bowl of hot soup will have you sprinting to our basement toilet!"

LOCATION: TOKYO, JAPAN
CREDIT: KIDO

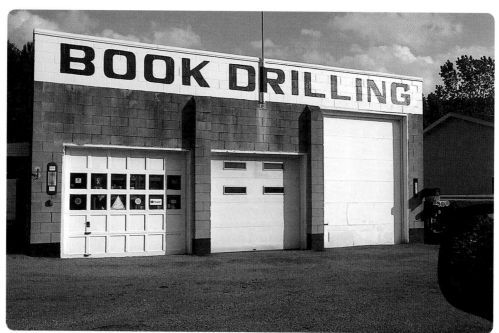

LOCATION: NEW CASTLE, PENNSYLVANIA, USA   CREDIT: ERIC BROOKS

Finally, a lucrative new revenue stream for book publishers!

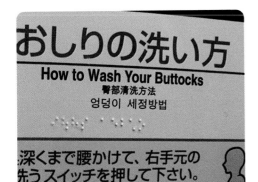

LOCATION: TOKYO, JAPAN   CREDIT: AARON D. ALBRECHT

We care deeply about your buttocks.

LOCATION: HALLABAT, JORDAN   CREDIT: JESSICA LEE

All shepherds are kindly requested
to tend to their flocks within the stipulated
flocking area.

LOCATION: TURKEY   CREDIT: EDWARD JESS

渚でやろう。

Please do it at the beach.

ホームの端は危険です。白線の内側でお待ちください。
The platform edge is dangerous.
Please wait behind the white line.

LOCATION: TOKYO, JAPAN   CREDIT: EMMANUEL CANAAN

Short on water and logic.

By "it," I presume they mean staring at a woman getting a stomach massage while drinking.

LOCATION: CROOKHAVEN, IRELAND   CREDIT: STEFAN WRBA

Once you pick your speed limit, you have to stick with it.

LOCATION: COLUMBUS, WISCONSIN, USA   CREDIT: CINDEE BOWEN

Maybe the cops should put up the following sign: "We have fingerprint kits and can use them on giant black letters."

LOCATION: CAPETOWN, SOUTH AFRICA   CREDIT: JONATHAN HAHN

Why wouldn't your illegally parked car be fine? Don't worry about that menacing barbed wire—we promise we won't so much as touch your illegally parked car sitting here on our private property.

LOCATION: SANTA CRUZ, CALIFORNIA, USA   CREDIT: ELIZABETH IVANOVICH

Just $150? No problem. Put it on my credit card.

LOCATION: MILWAUKEE, WISCONSIN, USA   CREDIT: JEFF NIEHUS

Hey, kids, great news!

请勿跨越
PLEASE DON'T SPAN
超えるべからず

LOCATION: BEIJING, CHINA   CREDIT: CHRIS TOWNSEND

It must be tough for the locals to put up with all of our spanning.
If only we knew what the hell it was so we could stop doing it.

USE THE QUEEN TO INVITE POWERFUL WATER

LOCATION: SHANGHAI, CHINA   CREDIT: MARKUS LINDAHL

Please, O Great Queen, I summon you now to bring forth your powerful water.

LOCATION: ROCKY MOUNTAIN NATIONAL PARK, COLORADO, USA   CREDIT: JOE MCDANIEL

LOCATION: GUILIN, CHINA   CREDIT: CODY FROCK LEE

Nominee for understatement of the year.

When God gives someone the finger . . .

LOCATION: BEIJING, CHINA   CREDIT: MICHAEL HIGGINS

Nice to get a warning. I suppose the alternative is "Ohshitthathurt."

LOCATION: ASWAN, EGYPT   CREDIT: CLAUDIA RAVE

No using crossed legs to keep pants dry.

LOCATION: JAIPUR, INDIA   CREDIT: ALISON PICHER

LOCATION: AUGUSTA, MAINE, USA   CREDIT: DARWIN STANTON

Hmmm. Wonder who's been spreading all those STDs.

Talk about overcoming obstacles.

LOST IN TRANSLATION

Ah, technology . . . the answer to our lingual impasse. Or is it? Google Translate offers a free tool to all—and some may be tempted to use it. If so, that might account for at least a small percentage of the signs in this book. As a little experiment, I used Google to translate Hamlet's famous soliloquy—first into Hungarian. Then I took the Hungarian text and translated that into Urdu. I translated the Urdu version into Vietnamese and then the Vietnamese version into Hebrew and then the Hebrew version into French and the French version back into English. Not surprisingly, things got a bit lost in Google translation . . .

Hungarian to Urdu to Vietnamese to Hebrew to French to English via Google Translate
What you get: can not, or this issue:
Freedom of nobler mind games in
Slings, arrows outrageous statements,
A firearm in a sea of pain or
Contrary to their end? But die
No, at the end of a dream, said
heart attack, and thousands of natural shocks
Pinky, we have already signed

Do not be surprised. Sleep die
Changed: Perhaps the dream: Yes, apply;
These capabilities, What Dreams May Come
He was a pear when the coil weight

The Original
To be, or not to be: that is the question:
Whether 'tis nobler in the mind to suffer
The slings and arrows of outrageous fortune,
Or to take arms against a sea of troubles,
And by opposing end them? To die: to sleep;
No more; and by a sleep to say we end
The heart-ache and the thousand natural shocks
That flesh is heir to, 'tis a consummation
Devoutly to be wish'd. To die, to sleep;
To sleep: perchance to dream: ay, there's the rub;
For in that sleep of death what dreams may come
When we have shuffled off this mortal coil

Danger

Park closed
due to
hazardous
trees

BCParks

LOCATION: CATHEDRAL GROVE, BRITISH COLUMBIA, CANADA   CREDIT: MARCIA DEANS

Normally the trees are pretty tame, but every so often they turn against the park visitors.

LOCATION: HONG KONG   CREDIT: CASPER WANDEL

Could be any noise, really. But it will happen suddenly, without any pre-noise to tell you when the actual noise will arrive.

LOCATION: COLOGNE, GERMANY   CREDIT: PATRICK SMITH

Hey, kids, forget Disney. Grab your little shovels—we're going to Wormland this year!

LOCATION: FORT MEYERS, FLORIDA, USA   CREDIT: JERRY MICKELSON

Five out of three bankers consider this to be an actual bank.

LOCATION: CHISEKESI, ZAMBIA   CREDIT: BJÖRN LINDQVIST

Turn right for repressive dictatorship.

BEWARE OF
OPPOSITE
RIGHT TURNERS

小心迎面
右轉車輛

LOCATION: KOWLOON, CHINA   CREDIT: TOM GEE

Also beware of the opposite of people who write succinctly.

LOCATION: TRINIDAD   CREDIT: PATRICK SMITH

A perfectly natural name for a truck.

LOCATION: CHIAPAS, MEXICO CREDIT: MAUD JOHANSSON

Bet you've been wondering what those giant green things are on either side of the road.

Foot Owner's Guide
- **Wearing Instructions**
- **Break In**
- **Care**

LOCATION: BLOOMINGTON, INDIANA, USA   CREDIT: COURTNEY CLAYTON

And to think I've been wearing my feet without instructions all these years.

LOCATION: CAIRO, EGYPT   CREDIT: PATRICK SMITH

All schmuck, all the time. It's a schmuck collector's dream come true.

LOCATION: KUALA-LUMPUR, MALAYSIA   CREDIT: ANDERS SVEDMYR

LOCATION: DELHI, INDIA   CREDIT: PATRICK SMITH

In other words, the only way to avoid more shops is if you never move.

Whatever sexual hang-ups you may have, please, my friend, share them with me.

LOCATION: FUCKING, AUSTRIA   CREDIT: MICHAEL BARLETT

Finally, a way to explain abstinence that young people can understand.

LOCATION: KNYSNA, SOUTH AFRICA   CREDIT: NELIA GUNN

Part of their new exercise regiment.

LOCATION: NOSY BE, MADAGASCAR   CREDIT: SASKIA FLIEK

Could the sign maker be any more graphic about what he doesn't want us to do?

私らしく、あなたらしく

LOCATION: TOYKO, JAPAN   CREDIT: LYNN SCHNEIDER

Competing for world's sluttiest city center?

LOCATION: BOULDERS BEACH, SOUTH AFRICA   CREDIT: HOLLY NELSON

Sorry, the penguin meet-and-greet has been canceled.

NOTE FROM THE AUTHOR

I started photographing funny signs when, like many of you, I was caught off guard by a few signs during my travels. Now, seventeen years later, I've received about 40,000 sign photos from travelers. Hard to believe, but there are great new ones coming in every day.

There are so many great signs that have not yet been photographed, and with new signs going up every day, the only way to gather them is with an army of travelers. In other words, you. Thank you for continuing to send in signs, rate the signs that others have submitted, and write your own funny captions for them at Signspotting.com.

If you like the Signspotting books, you may also enjoy the following:

The Exhibit: The Signspotting Project
Please keep your eyes open for "The Signspotting Project"—one of the funniest exhibits you'll ever see. We have enlarged more than one hundred of the wackiest sign photos

and mounted them back onto real metal signs at approximately life size and put them all on display in the center of cities around the world—free to the public. At the global launch of the exhibit in Stockholm, it became the biggest attraction in the city with 30,000 daily visitors. To see if any of these events are coming your way, check www.signspotting .com/events.

The Keynote: Doug Lansky speaks to travelers as well as travel industry and marketing professionals. As a noted travel writer and author who has hosted a travel show for the Discovery Channel and filed regular reports for NPR's *Savvy Traveler*, Doug has put together an inspirational, practical, and funny presentation for university students and independent travelers about planning a postgraduate trip around the world (how to save thousands of dollars, travel safely, and custom-make an itinerary to find the most enriching experiences). He also gives entertaining and insightful presentations to tourism professionals about destination marketing campaigns that have gone wrong and how to prevent it from happening. And his talk for marketing professionals, "The Art of Miscommunication," uses entertaining examples of failed campaigns to show the key crossroads where branding disasters occur so they can best be prevented. To book Doug for an upcoming event, visit www.kepplerspeakers.com.